Give Me the Word

Laura Merzig Fabrycky

GIVE ME
THE WORD

Advent and Other Poems, 2000-2015

for Nilo,
with gratitude

Laura M. F

Saar River Press

"Almonds" and "Finished" appeared previously in *Glass* (vol. 4, no.1). "On a Donkey," "Humble Access," and "Wilderness Triptych" appeared previously in TFCA's *The Current*.

Cover Art: *Parting Hence Away* by Jan Aiello, http://aiellojan.wix.com/janramseyaiello

Cover Design: Ricky Altizer, http://www.rickyaltizer.com

ISBN: 0692571833
ISBN-13: 978-0692571835

Library of Congress Control Number: 2015918760
Saar River Press, Annandale, Virginia

For my grandmother,
Beatrice Gage Merzig

Contents

III   Words in Other Lands

I first encountered one of Laura's poems twelve or thirteen years ago in my mailbox, its envelope slipped in among a dozen others. It was almost Christmas, and our mail brought the smiling faces of friends with new spouses or newborn babies, beneath cheery greetings like PEACE ON EARTH and JOY JOY JOY! But tucked into Laura's card I found—printed, trimmed to size, discreet, unassuming—an Advent poem.

Each December another followed.

I have my own annual writerly tradition, a tightly constructed, double-sided Christmas letter that seeks by any available means to avoid the banalities of the genre and render my quite ordinary life (how shall I put this?) *fascinating.* I try to resist the cataloguing impulse—travels, home renovations, job promotions, babies—and yet to distill a year in my family's life to a few hundred words. It isn't easy, yet I persevere in this vision.

So each year I energetically, or at times resignedly, send off my letter, and await Laura's poem in return. When it arrives, I savor it like a delicacy.

Here, amidst the glut of images in our Christmas mail, is text, but not mere text: art, craft, words evoking images of another kind— primitive, hand-drawn, colored in softer hues, inching slowly across a rugged terrain. Here are peasants and farm animals, prophets and kings, types and shadows, and inevitably their fulfillment: the mother with her ordinary, extraordinary child. Contours of faith and doubt, hope and despair, always tinged—like a breath caught, held—with wonder.

"I wonder...." one of my children might begin, usually when we're in the car, and then proceed with a question about the dietary habits of teacup pigs, say, or the time it would take the Blue Angels to orbit Jupiter. Before the first child is finished another interrupts with, "Mom, ask Siri!"

A brief verbal scuffle ensues over which child will hold my iPhone and whisper the question into Siri's solicitous ear. Then picture the result: infinitude of information summoned with the tap of a finger—breath caught, held, and slowly released to the inevitable flattening disappointment of Yahoo! Answers or Wikipedia.

The predictability of the exchange bores me, but not as much as the long-term result distresses me. For all their brilliant convenience, our devices short-circuit the investigative process, diminish the imagination, and hold out the false promise of human omniscience.

I wonder if we have lost our capacity for wonder, in both senses of the word: the pondering of speculative questions, and the act of marveling.

Surely the Incarnation of Christ deserves no less than the wide-eyed slack-jawed posture of awe. Yet two thousand years after the event, we are more removed from it than ever—not just by time, but by strata of luxury and activity and excess; by news cycle, blogosphere, and social media; by Siri.

If, in spite of it all, we manage to protect a sliver of time and solitude for reflection—if we abjure frenetic Martha, channel placid Mary instead—then a new danger arises. A vapor of sentimentality threatens to obscure the brute realities. On my mantel, hand-carved wooden figures cluster about the manger, shepherds, beasts, and Magi bowed down in adoration. "The cattle are lowing, the poor baby wakes, but little Lord Jesus no crying he makes." It is the very loveliness of the familiar images and turns of phrase that risks rendering the earth-shattering miracle of the Incarnation something sweet. A children's story, nothing more.

But I suspect the reality was otherwise: dirt, blood, slimy afterbirth and stench of manure. Homelessness, desperation, and shame (she would always be remembered, by some, as the girl who got knocked up by God-knows-who). The wise men's indiscreet questions that gave rise to the flight to Egypt and the slaughter of other women's infant sons. The harrowing fear, heart-wrenching loss—and always, the dim memory of a Promise, like the thin ribbon of dawn illuminating the inky horizon.

The Man of Sorrows was born to a people of sorrows—a people vanquished and scattered, re-gathered and subdued, occupied and overtaxed and left, for four hundred years, without prophet or mouthpiece or Word; *a people walking in darkness.* This fact, amidst our well-intended preparations and treasured Christmas traditions, we risk forgetting. And in forgetting, we may miss the greatness of the good news he preached—liberty to the captives, comfort to the grieving, the binding up of the broken hearted; the year of the Lord's favor, the day of God's vengeance, the building up of the ancient ruins.

Forgiveness granted, redemption accomplished, but not in a way anyone could have dreamed.

Laura's poems are an invitation to wonder—to lean forward in speculation, stand back in awe. They are an invitation to re-imagine the first Advent. Like the lines of a quick pencil-sketch, like thick bold layers of oil paint, they both strip away and fill in, challenging us to behold afresh the Incarnation in its simplicity and infinite complexity, its meanness and beauty, its ordinary humanness and its ineffable divinity.

To scan a poem is to fundamentally mishandle it. A good one arrests you—forces you back into your seat; demands to be re-read, absorbed, pondered. It conjures, kindles, expands in the mind. "For poetry too," wrote C.S. Lewis in *Reflections on the Psalms*, "is a little incarnation, giving body to what had before been invisible and inaudible."

This is what Laura's poems have been to me through the years: little incarnations, arriving every December, just when I needed them most.

Heather Ferngren Morton

Deep winter chill, full of quiet, surrounded the waiting commuters on the Metro station platform in Silver Spring, Maryland. It was here, fifteen years ago, that I suddenly became aware of our collective, attentive waiting. Many of us commuters gazed blankly down the rail, our ears tuned to hear the clatter of an approaching train. Others kept their eyes pinned to the lights embedded in the concrete platform, waiting for the subtle blink that would signal the train's arrival. Without fanfare, we had adopted Advent's posture: watching, listening, waiting.

We were just commuters trying to get somewhere, but stuck waiting for something to happen; for someone else to make it happen. When the train finally delivered me to Washington, D.C., I took a few minutes at my desk to write a poem about that moment of wonder and observation. I could not see then that this small moment of "entering in" would grow into an annual writing tradition, reflecting on the biblical account of the Incarnation.

Most of these Advent poems went out on little printed papers, hand-scissored to size, and tucked into our family's annual Christmas cards or digitally pasted on the holiday e-cards we would send when we were living abroad.

It has taken me a very long time, and with the patient encouragement of family and friends, to let these poems be out and about more in the world, letting them traverse more freely on their own. I'm a mother that likes to hold firmly to my children's hands, and a poet that is inclined to do the same with my poems. But I have learned to find joy in seeing them venture out, hoping that all that has been poured into them will endure, that they will be received with love and grace, that their presence will bring a measure of goodness to the world, and that they will be bettered by others.

I surely have. I am honored that my friend Heather Morton, a skilled writer and wise observer who cultivates her own Christmastime writing tradition, provided a foreword to this collection. My good fortune multiplied when the very gifted Jan Aiello agreed to grace the cover with her art, and yet again, abundantly, when Ricky Altizer agreed, with his considerable skills, to orchestrate the parts into a beautiful whole. I am so grateful for each of them and for their talents.

These Advent poems (and their few Christmastide siblings) have grown to a small collection. But since fifteen or so collected poems seemed like a very small offering, I included many more that grew from the humus of my life, both in the United States and in our years abroad. These include both poems I wrote as an American foreigner observing everyday life in other countries, as well as poems from the early years of the Arab Spring (beginning in Tunisia in December 2010, gaining strength across the region in 2011), a time of dizzying hope that in many nations was violently crushed, leaving a residue of thick despair and on-going suffering in many parts.

These poems represent my own years of making: sense, beauty, connection, meaning, and translation. Each attempts to offer something true, if difficult. That is the task of a poet—*making* (or *poiéma*, in Greek). It's quite practical work.

This collection is dedicated to Beatrice Gage Merzig, my grandmother, a woman of remarkable talents, intelligence, lifelong faith, and her own poetic sensibilities. Grandma Bea wrote a poem long before I was born about old Thornwood—a beloved family cabin that tragically burned down, the fire taking with it what felt like a good era—and the artless insurer's report after the fact. The poem still sings, as good poems always will, and it tells an important story. I honor the imprint of Grandma Bea's life on my own and on our extended family.

I am especially grateful for my husband, David, who has exhorted and supported me in so many ways, and takes my poetry-making quite seriously, which is a gift I do not take for granted; our children, who are themselves ineffable living poems but who still ask, nonetheless, to be named fully and clearly here: Miriam Leslie Fabrycky, Hannah Corbly Fabrycky, and (whose interests are being represented presently by his older sisters) Adam John Fabrycky. And I am very grateful for my parents, Jack and Babs Merzig, and for their good idea of making this collection. I love you all, more than any artfully arranged words could adequately convey.

I also thank Emunah Arak Rankin, Lindsay Hutter, Nancy Ziegler, and Maggie Johns; my writing group (Jan Aiello, Michelle DeCarlo, Leslie Egge, Stephanie Norquist, Lori Borg, and, not least, Heather Morton); and the many kind friends —here unnamed but not unacknowledged—who read or listened, and asked for more.

Laura Merzig Fabrycky
All Saints' Day 2015

Give Me the Word

Observations on the Platform

I.

I keep breathing.
It takes me by surprise:
The very sustenance that we require,
what swirls around us,
demands that we take it in.

Along the gray railway platform,
fellow travelers digest the chill,
puffs of white nostril-steam.
We all like oxen breathe away,
listening.
("No, I did hear a whistle! I think the train is
coming.")
Surrounded by the air,
working at this winter-process of ours—
our making clouds, that is.

We make our clouds,
busily oblivious
that we are given to listening and breathing.

II.

We have always been waiting,
and not knowing,
longing with tears for the One Who Comes—
The One Who Comes Who Breathes,
and Who Listens.
Who stands along the gray railway platform
among we all like oxen, we all, the sheep gone
astray.
The One Who Makes the Clouds

in the sky
and in the lungs of creatures.
Who will work too at this winter-task with us.

The One Who is Not the Clouds,
but Who is Everywhere, Swirling Around Us
Yet Who is Not Contained.
The very sustenance that we require:
present that we may take him in.

Silver Spring, Maryland
Advent 2000

4

O heart's desire, my longings clothe me.
At watch, I stand with open upturned hands
Near the door frame of our empty chamber,
Trusting that I will glimpse your radiance
In the daybreak of your appearing.
Purify my fear. I reach for your hem.
Holy root of Jesse, the key of David,
Only in your sheepfold do I find pasture.
Neither before thee was any like thee—
Star of the morning, Wisdom, Emmanuel.

Object Lesson: Swaddling Clothes

This telling detail:
> how the youngest bear witness
> from the start.
Mary wraps her son—
> he left the snug, overshadowed womb,
> entering the world with arms
> that startle and flail
> by nascent instinct.
The youngest bear witness
> in their bodies that
> the bottom has dropped,
> the ground shifts and gives way,
> earth akimbo, creation spinning,
> the reeling disorient,
>> and falling, falling
We are all falling. The youngest
> bear witness, and he does the same.
> Arms splay into the void.
So Mary wraps her son—
> it's too soon to stretch out his arms.
> The first-born of all creation,
> wound tight, spiceless,
> becalmed.

Advent 2014

What the Chronicler Remembered

Final trumpet blasts,
      a flurry of holy dance,
            shouted amens,
the ark celebrated and retired to its tent.
David returned to bless his
household of cedar.

Reclining secure,
David's thoughts wandered
to the tent.
            (A wave of royal pity?)
Thus
he summoned Nathan,
the prophet.

"Look at me in my luxury,
while the ark of the covenant
is out in that tent."

Overawed, or curiously unlistening,
Nathan spoke too soon,
delivering a prophecy *pro forma*:
"God is with you. Do what is in your heart."

By night the Word of the Lord came to Nathan:
"Listen, prophet, and tell this king:
You will not build me a house.
Recall, king, that I have moved with my people
tent to tent, shelter to shelter.
The foundation of my great name
bears the weight of these mighty cedars
that now shelter you.
I took you from among the sheep in the fields,
and placed you on this gilded throne.

7

I have subdued your enemies.

"This is the word:
That house, O king, is yet to be built,
for I will build that house from your very lineage.
A child from your line will emerge,
and he shall be my builder
and the cornerstone.
A tender shoot,
his rule,
a kingdom unshakeable.
He will call me Father,
and I will call him
Beloved Son."

Thus, having heard,
Nathan returned to deliver the message
to King David, who then,
in awe, blessed the Lord.

Annandale, Virginia
Advent 2013

Naming on the Eighth Day

What majestic slow unfurling
        this king was given,
        even if custom made it so.

The holy parents holding in their hearts
        the gift of the angel,
        and obedience to the gift.

Awed, hushed meditation on the life
        gurgling before them:
        a week-old baby,

The Word enfleshed and exhausting
        in all the happy ways,
        suspended in quiet time,

In baby thighs and layers of chin,
        nursing day and night,
        an established feeding schedule—

New and yet Ever.

A perfect week.
        The seventh day, he rests
        his head on Mary's bosom, unnamed.

Quietness before the coming storm.

He was never their own, although
        for a week, it seemed he was.
        Rhythms of a little life,

The Named from the Beginning.
        On the eighth day, Mary and Joseph arise

to declare the Name: God Saves.

Now unfurled and unleashed,
        they hasten to the Temple,
        the simple, holy week eclipsed.

Amman, Jordan
Advent 2012

"This move was a fulfillment of the prophetic words, 'He shall
be called a Nazarene.'" (Matt. 2:22–23)

It was not simple mimesis
    that he was born under the mantle Nazarite.
It was mantle, whole-cloth.

The angels and prophets foresaw
    Joseph's move of his family to Nazareth.
    (Mary was a Tzippori girl, so this was a return
    to the familiar.)

Long ago, another promised son,
    born under a mantle to save—
    born far from Nazareth town, and yet a
Nazarene.
His lips were consecrated,
    forbidden to taste wine or strong drink,
    yet he would quaff the delicacies of women,
    disoriented by their honeyed ways of deceit.
He flirted with violence. Nations swooned.

In apparent defeat,
    the Nazarenes would spread wide
    their arms and lay their hands on the marbled
    pillars of the world,
    pillorying their stage props of power,
    rending their purple dressings in two.

Born judges under the mantle,
    whose self-gifts in death
    surprised longing, weary
    hearts.

Domus, Civitas, Imperium

A fragile start, indeed—
    a stunning miscalculation, some would say:
    this smattering of sparks,
    tossed like drops of water onto arid ground.
Dissipation; preposterous emissaries:

To the *Domus*, a maiden—
    Betrothed, but no more,
    her improbable claim raising the wise eyebrows
    of the securely fruitful women,
    they who rule that sphere with their own, more
    hidden powers.

To the *Civitas*, shepherds—
    No cultured eye beheld the angel armies in their
    starry array; no bard, no poet.
    Sheep-sitters with no mind, or words, for
    stellar spectacle, and little else to gird their
    public testimony.

To the *Imperium*, distant kings—
    They who long abandoned their realms of
    potentia to seek, in service, a greater one. What
    king—*what king worth his salt, anyway*—pursues
    another without sword drawn?

Amman, Jordan
Advent 2011

12

Lord, you have given me
no words,
and even on the eve of
the arrival of all hope,
I am without words.
Please—
don't leave me empty
tonight.
I scan the horizon
for a star, and ask you to guide me,
in the meantime, in the dark.
I watch,
again,
expecting you still.
Give me the Word,
if not the words.

St. George's Cathedral Pilgrim Guest House
Nablus Road, Jerusalem
Christmas Eve, 2010

A Penitential Advent

We do not gnash our teeth
but we certainly clench them.
A people waking and walking in darkness—
stumble grumble mumble—
honk our horns, disgusted, at the bright light:
slowing our traffic to a crawl.
Our hasty attempts at living,
thwarted.
We will be slowed down,
or we will drown.

We who walk in darkness know
that darkness.
   We know it better than light:
how our love is so laced with hate,
our expectations undisciplined and unruly.
Choking anger, exhaust of unquenched wills—
bumble fumble tumble—

The light is rising and is already risen.
Curved on ourselves, we are now bent back,
new orbits to trace and travel.
We know the darkness of our own gravity,
the black holes we make of ourselves.
      We know that.
We need this light. We need it to shine,
burning through the darkness and looking
behind and through our shadows,
and telling us the truth about ourselves,
standing us up straight and looking out,
so that we may more clearly see
this Great Light.

        Falls Church, Virginia
        2009

14

In Grief (for Anna W.)

Mary whispers:
You do not know what is in me,
to what ends I'll go to keep you safe.
How I long, as all mothers do, to quiet
the madness of this world,
to stand between evil and your life
to lay this old body down for you;
not yours for mine.
But the strength of my will finally reaches an end,
finite and frail.
My arms may be strong,
but there *are* powers greater than me.
The life given in you must be spent
as all lives must be.
Yet, as I live, I know,
that there is no power greater than you,
Little One.
So rest, for the night comes when
I will not be able to hold you.
But tonight, I will.

2008

The Dreams of a Weeping Prophet

A long time ago,
Jeremiah the Weeping Prophet fell asleep.
His leg twitched in slumber.
And the word of God overshadowed him—

Wailing, weeping women tormented in Ramah.
The children lie in pieces along the road.
Frightened by a baby, a king is driven to slaughter.
Rachel shrugs off comfort, and the only safety
is found in Egypt, the place of captivity.

But look! Light shines out of darkness!
New wine and oil, here and there, our Lord gathers
his flock.
The harlot becomes a virgin.
The indescribable new thing: the inscrutable
welling up within the mother-virgin.
A woman bears God, swollen with divinity!

The Weeper woke from sleep,
pressed but not crushed,
perplexed, persecuted, struck down,
but not destroyed.

2001

Arabia Felix!

When the caravan threaded through the gates of
Jerusalem, the troubles of Herod coursed
through the streets of the city.
They had not come to worship him;
their camels ladened with treasure were
reserved for another king.
The utterances of prophets concerning
humble Bethlehem—
these ancient words now invaded the empire,
stealth and fury,
and lit the sky with fire
along the utter reaches of the spice road.
Months before, the incense trees
along the southern-most coast
had poured their gracious sap from their wounds,
tuned to the tree-shepherd's song,
trunk-tears to burn worshipfully for this baby.
Arabia Felix! and its gifts:
From Persia, now arrived to Jerusalem.

Doha, Qatar
after a trip to Muscat, Oman
2007

The poetry of Mary's heart
and Simeon's stark and adoring words
seemed far removed
when the quotidian rhythms of "life with baby"
set in.
Joseph returned to work.
Mary resettled the family into their Nazareth home.

Jesus slept.
    ("Finally in a proper place," Mary sighed, folding
laundry.)

Wondrous incarnation,
let us now kneel to observe
the first divine coo, babble, and gurgle.
Marvel at God the Word drooling
saliva and milk,
issuing his first (social) smile.
He will soon steady his wobbling head
and he will reach to grab a tendril of Mary's hair.

O Holy Sight!

Alexandria, Virginia
2006

Even when I did not know you,
I hoped and longed for you
with such painful expectation
that it produced taste in my mouth
when I had not eaten,
and fire in my belly
when I had not known passion.
And it was precisely this surprise—
having when I did not possess,
knowing when I had not been known—
that at times I wondered
if this movement was simply a matter of
my dreams:
hysteria.
Even my barrenness was beyond my knowledge,
when I learned that I was bearing fruit.
My ancestor, Hannah, prayed my drunken prayers
for me
before I knew how to pray them.
And within me now, I bear the longing
of those who equally do not know
that they likewise long.

Bishop Payne Library
Virginia Theological Seminary
Alexandria, Virginia
2005

Nunc Dimittis

Old pious Simeon told me that night
What G-d had told him,
And like Sarah our Ancestor
I laughed to hear him say it,
and dismissed him, saying,
"So to you, after these four hundred years
of Divine Silence—
to *you*, old Simeon, has been said,
that you will not die until you see Israel's Messiah?"
Preposterous! His jokes!
"So, my friend, rest easy, for you shall never die!"

Years passed since I had laughed at Simeon,
though we saw each other every day or so
in the city.
But the day he disappeared,
I saw him running through the streets of Jerusalem,
robes hoisted—
as if outrunning a king's chariot, or hastening to a
lost son—
heading toward the temple.
I called out to him,
"Would that I knew that pleasure at your age,
Simeon!" On his heels were tongues of flame.

It was said among the neighbors that he did not die,
but that a flaming chariot bore him up
like Elijah the prophet.
Righteous old Simeon, how he waited for
consolation.

Silver Spring, Maryland
2004

20

Elizabeth—great with child and seized by the
Spirit—
Greeted the mother of her Lord.
And just as the icon of their embrace
formed in the eternal mind's eye,
the old woman had to sit
as the child within her flipped about.
Mary let out her *Magnificat* as she rubbed
Elizabeth's feet, fat and full from pregnancy.
For three months these two lived
on the cusp of the revolution.
As the children within them grew,
so too grew the fullness of time,
the near crest of the wave of coming justice.
At night the young woman Mary saw visions
and the old woman Elizabeth dreamed dreams.
Next to her Zechariah groaned in sleep,
a man full of prophecy yet unable to speak.
In the morning
Mary and Elizabeth went to the market.
Mary giggled as she helped Elizabeth make way
for her burgeoning belly.
Later, in the kitchen,
Mary sensed that the child within her would be
very great.
Her womb could not hold him in.
Piercing her wonder, Elizabeth called from another
room—
would Mary check on the baking bread and take
some to Zechariah?
Mary—whose *Fiat* tore the sky—reached for the
loaf and cut a slice, carrying it to Elizabeth's silent
husband.
These three servants—

the believing and the unbelieving,
they of the here and not yet,
moving in the mystery of the just-breaking Day.

Advent 2003

Shutting out the ash and haze and fury
and the cacophonous blur—
baying, honking, laughing—
Mary tucks her young one into bed
and slips outside to gaze at the nighttime sky.
This strange land has received them.
Pyramids tower on the horizon, symbols of slavery.
Here her people were not welcome;
dogs—all of them, until one young boy found
safety drifting among the river's reeds.
And now tucked away like her child,
she with her husband Joseph
wait for news that the fire has gone out,
that Herod no longer seeks to slaughter her baby.
What a strange land we walk through.
Could the Nile carry him to safety too?

Advent 2002

Years of Making

Leaves fall now
In brisk direction,
Down.

A thousand pinpricks
Of sound,
Around.

The cardinal queen
In the rosebud
Found

Dried bean pods.
Leafless rustle. Food
Abounds.

Blue so clean,
The sky sighs clouds,
Profound.

Curbside leaf bundles,
Suburban haystacks,
Bound.

Blackbird on a limb,
My heart
Pounds.

2015

The Dunn Holly

That hedge on the western edge of the plot is so
necessary in keeping out the riff-raff, maintaining
our sense of civilization. The neighbors are
marvelous people, really. I bring them a baked
good from time to time, often around the holidays.
Neighbors do this.

But they'll also observe me—
and I don't care that they do—
from their kitchen window studiously working on
the hedge between us.

                          One holly bush in the border
drill line—*we thought it was a line of boxwood, like*
what lines the driveway of the old mansion nearby
(but no, it's not that classy)—
is all dunn-up:
                    all brown and dead and
standing there like a kid in gym class
                        that forgot his sneakers,
or like the black kid from eighth grade who died
from a heart condition, and they announced it over
the intercom when we were in drama class.

We stopped mid-way through a scene in which
the hero says, "Dead for a ducat, dead!"
followed by a sword-thrust into an imaginary
curtain, our action cut off
by a well-adjusted voice from the speaker box
high up on the wall above the metal rim of the
bulletin board.
As sober-minded as eighth graders can try to be,
still we couldn't imagine what a heart condition
was, much less death.

		I over-identified with the news,
wanted to align myself to it, wanted to hop into the
dunn-colored drama of his death. "Of course, I
knew him. I can't believe this has happened."
In truth, I wasn't confident who we were
talking about and forgot his name
almost immediately after it was uttered
from the box,
the abrupt click-off of the intercom like
a one-gun salute,
startled middle-schoolers standing blankly at
attention.

		Months later, they went ahead and
printed his picture in the yearbook,
a morbid placeholder.
(I guess no one remembered to tell the printing
company. Might have been nice to put in a small
tribute, or at least *an end date*.)
His closed-mouth smile stood in the row between
MacQuillin and McSwiggen,
a bold dead brown Martin
in that line of living green.

			I aim to prune it all out,
but the line won't rejigger, the hedgerow won't fill
in, *will it?* The rest of the bushes, green, will
remain inert like ruminant beasts, all dumb in the
eyes:
		eighth graders practicing a scene of
Shakespeare, unintelligible at the foggy,
dim-witted hour of two o'clock in the afternoon,
thrusting swords into Lord Poloniuses hiding
behind the arrases on the stage edge;

29

me with my pruning shears, plunged into
the necessary curtain that hangs between
civilization and the encroaching wilderness,
making work of that dunn holly
in time for the holidays.

2015

Marcescence

Out the window,
the pin oak in the frigid air
still clings with fingertips
to her withered leaves.
They are dead,
and still she clings.

I have borne a child.
As I bathe, or brush,
I draw out with my fingers
hair that now refuses to stay
rooted to my scalp.
A flower that has fruited,
my petals fall.
Few discuss this postnatal abscission.
Yet, here it is: with fingers,
I rake my hair.

It is Lent.
My friend tells me that
our neighborhood is suffocating her.
"I feel like I'm just fighting
to keep ten percent of me alive,
when I could be living fully somewhere else."
But what if even *that*
has to die?

I see the pin oak in the stiff breeze,
still clutching fast her dead leaves,
against the bluing night sky,
and I am entirely sympathetic.

Ilda
2015

31

Dew

Up the bank of grass,
and right up to
the brick path of the elementary school,
the sun peaks over the distant, leafy canopy,
illuminating ten million
watery jewels of morning.
As we walk, before the bell's last call,
I tell my children to take it all
in, admire the handiwork,
and give honor that is
due the maker of grass—
moreover, each individual blade—
and, as to us his daily bread,
see his heart's token for each one
as much as the whole:
No matter the weather ahead,
each blade, this day,
has received a drink.

Iva Lane
2015

Tattered Sail

It floats mid-air,
lashed to the masts of the gray garbage can
and the bush with no name,
a tattered sail,
spun by the daddy longlegs
that have made their home
on the east side of the house.

It moves in the breeze,
a massive gossamer mouth
in the earnest
roundness of a caroler.

In its center a lightning bug,
an insect bull's-eye,
a pantry stocked for a journey
on the wind, itself a gateway,
a hole into and between
worlds, a sail on a ship
aloft on the churning waves
of another world, shipwrecked
on the shores of our own.

Tuesday is trash day.
I'll give it all of Monday to sail
as far as it can.

33

A First Taste of Death

Spindly, rippling fuzz
  in smooth and stately
  'callapidda' gallop
along the curbside,
adventuring crusader of a thing:
  We are spellbound by its
  hard-earned distance.
Cheering its advance,
  adopting his imagined life
        into ours.

We reach into his life gently
  tickled by his young bristles,
as if petting a fish beneath the water's surface.
Real distance between species—
  fascinated wonder—bordered—
  restrained
  by respect.

The foolish boys have hastened to
  our perch at the curb;
drawn by our hunched peering and watchfulness.
And with an unthoughtful stomp,
  one snuffs out our caterpillar's life.

Off
  they
    run.

There was no border there.
Real death issued by the boot of a boy
who
  never
    thought

anything of it at all.

And she for whom I would die
   has bunched her small, thick hands
   over her eyes,
her mouth has opened to a silent cry
   and she is tasting the pain of love
   in the face of death.

——meaningless.

Now we are searching for another
callapidda.
And we find ten, twelve, more,
all inching in helpless formation towards
that precarious stretch
where
     as a mother
I draw fervently upon my faith in
the redemption of the world.

Al-Hashemiyeen Street
2010

Balloon

We had been so careful with its properties.
Preserved by the cold,
the forgotten balloon in the car still
floated with ambition.
Its treasured sister—remembered—
limp and weary from play.

Now, in the rainy drive to school,
one lies at our feet;
the other is stirring, nosing
the ceiling.
I am barking motherly orders, as doors open:
And out
      it
        flies.

She went racing to the clouds
before I could jump to grab
her slender white umbilical ribbon.
"God will shoot it down!" my three-year old
assures us.

It all happens so fast.
Even if the divine lets an arrow fly,
how will we know where it lands?

Falls Church, Virginia
2009

Formation

for M, H, and A

born with chisels
to an unmade mother,
you carved me,

formed my days
and nights, my
habits, thoughts, desires.

without your presence,
interruptions, and the
work you required

I would never
have learned to
walk and talk.

you took my
hand. we stumbled
together, and I

see now that
you formed me
and I you.

April 2015

No Name for This
for S.M., M.M., and A.W., M.W

We give name to our particular griefs,
but there is one that we do not even name.
Each grief is a precious pain,
yet we leave one in shadow.
You see,
an orphan awakens to a parentless horizon.
A widow, sleepily, reaches for her mate,
and finds an empty pillow.
A widower stares into
the pews at church and sees
pairs, like ducklings, and he is now
a lone drake.
But we have no name for this:
the mother from whom death has
snatched her child;
an empty lap.
A father who leans at the doorway
watching the hospice care of his dying son;
parents who stare at headstones that bear
years short and early,
who wonder why they not only bear the joyous life,
but now must tend the memory flame—
we have
no name for this.

Reflections en route from Detroit to Albany
for Papa, and the rest of us

The illumined parking lot—a neat box of orange
   matchstick fires
  from my airplane perch—
flickers in and out.   Then out.
Clouds erase them from view.
I am heading east, away from the dying sun
  and into the night.
The passengers behind me talk about their lives.
"I have some land in upstate New York."
"How lovely! Are there trees on your land?"
"Yes, it's quite wooded."
I turn off my reading lamp and look out into the dark.
I have some land in upstate New York too.
Wooded—yes, very.   Much more than I ever knew.
And now the lights are out.
Nothing to beware but the darkness now.
She in seat 8C says, "I think when you turn
  thirty, you become aware of dying."
No, I think.   Earlier than that.
Tonight, as I dream on this Detroit to Albany leg,
 the July fireworks have exploded in finality.
My hand has reached into the candy jar for a last furtive
    snack.
The ticking clock pendulum is stopped,
and we have made it down that long driveway.
I am looking out the backseat window,
Trying to catch the light from the cabin through
  the fast encroaching leaves.

midair, over the Midwest United States
2004

39

Viriditas

for Emunah, who gave me the word

We are sent into wildernesses
to carve out thirst,
to make eyes keen and hungry,
and to know
without shadows of doubt,
or despair, or suspicion,
that the flame is green,
the water is alive.
    Both are unstoppable and,
at once, orderly:
the crooked places are straightened
by the fluid plumb line;
the fire creates,
               awakens, and *skips*.
Up along the riverbanks,
the ferns reach their lovely hands
skyward,
purple heads emerge in the yellow winter straw,
a flash of green here and then there.
In the end, life.
The last word: *viriditas*.

Laetare Sunday
2015

40

Normal Service Resumes

The strike was fatal,
and therefore a success,
maybe his only in a good long while.
Whether he imagined himself
a black-and-white film damsel,
tied by a mustachioed villain
of despair, mesmerizing, cackling, tying
the rope tighter, we'll never know.
But that he lay down on the tracks
made, well,

      made the traffic horrible this morning.
It was *horrible*—
took hours for everyone to get to work;
a massive inconvenience,
that taking of life.
The company informs us
that normal service has resumed,
the wrinkle ironed away,
trains running smoothly
again.

July 2015

Jesus and Jonah

Jesus loved Jonah, that much is clear;
imitation flatters form.
Swallowed whole by the yawning
maw, earth and water—even that.
Then spat out, a victim triumphant.
But to such degree! Even asleep!
At the height of the raging storm!
Ballast and bait, flotsam and jetsam, swirl.
Jesus and Jonah, as if dead to the world,
roused by the panicked-to-death:
"Do you not care?" "What have you done?"
Both rise in the moment,
and with a word and a splash,
the seas becalm.

Falls Church, Virginia
2009

42

On the Trinity

Do you watch us
measure you,
slice and dice you,
and try to understand
relation and quiddity?
What an oddity y'all are!
Aquinas and the Speculatives have
spelunked thee,
yet I fear that we are still
only looking at shadows
on the cave wall.
I'd rather not threaten those
with any more of our kind of light.

2005

Humble Access

The gate is the needle's eye;
wedged, that I am, with camel's pride.
Kneeling, let me say this again—
Presume that I presume, even
as I do not presume.
This access is real, if
sublimely improbable.
But nothing is impossible with
God, as it is said,
so I will walk forward,
hands cupped,
tongue readied:
this is what will wash me.
Manifold goodness even to those of us
who run with our tails between our legs,
dogs of the bunch:
my worthiness is worthless here,
so please dwell in me, as I learn
to dwell in you.

Falls Church, Virginia
2009

you can slap it strike it
yell at it trip all over it
but the rock is
immoveable
an unbearable cup
foundational established strong
the cornerstone of the universe
the keystone of the world
rejected and overlooked
unsightly and inscrutable
no semblance to a garden paver out back
or a polished front porch-perched flagstone—

the way, there is no other way—

drink from the rock
drink ye all of it

2015

Learning to Hold a White Stone Gently

for the only one it could be for

These are the hard words.
    You would think they would be light and
    easy—
as I hear, for some, they are.

Not so for us.

These are the fearful words.
    Love poems—alabaster jars—should be
examined for integrity;
      it's a suspicious trade—
    at times dubious. I wish it were

Not so for us.

These are the true words:
      I will turn to a blank page
      as white as the dress I wore on
      the day you and I were wed;
    I will not leave it blank, nor can
      I return to that day.

I cannot return to that day, although
    in my mind, I turn it round and round
    like a white stone on a beach in Nice, where

    on our honeymoon, I already wondered if
      you longed for me,
    if you had re-centered to me as your
      fixed point.
    I picked up that honeymoon stone to remember.

The days became years,

and the stone
     moved through water, sand, fire,
     and
     now I take it in my hand to hold it
more truthfully, more gently,

as I wish these days and years had been for us.
     I had vowed to do so.

It will begin truthfully and hard,
     learning to hold a white stone gently.

Heifer, goat, and ram,
full-grown man and full-grown woman,
we lay with the animals in the hot sun.
This green earth and blue sky,
the grass around our ears:
breastbone and sternum
wishbones.

The crowd has gathered for the oblation,
to witness the cleaving and cleaving,
the covenant—
"Let me swear now:
Tear me apart in kind,"
split me in two;
cleave me.

"I bind unto myself this day,"
allow to pass between—
joints and marrow
soul and body
Man and Woman—
the furnace and the lamp:
riches and poverty
health and disease
joy and despair.

Tear me apart
rip my soul from my body
splice my joints from marrow,
if we—Man and Woman—are torn in two:
if I betray this covenant.

The sleep of divine ecstasy,
deep and dark,

abundant mystery: awe.
Righteous fear, expectant and pure,
We lay down our two halves before the crowd,
then our selves before the other.

And when it was dark
The flame passed between them.
Sealed upon their hearts,
branded,
torn and healed.

2002

Jane

I don't presume to know
what it felt like
in you.
You have given us some sense of it
in words, and
we'll let them stand as they are.

But I know what it feels like
in me—
how I cannot run fast enough to dodge it,
and why there is such solace to be found
in the day's chores:
bodily work
that refuses to be sensate,
but for which your arms and legs
feel, yes, so grateful.

Relieved for a time, a body says thank you
and says so in fatigue.
A dog settling on the wood floor
after a walk,
neck up, tongue out,
knees bent,
breathing hard,
quieted.

2013

Saturday Night in Early September

Sabbath descends with the night,
rolls in like a cloud, arrives upon
all the dirty dishes
on the counter, the inch of old milk
in the baby's bottle,
the near-empty bottle of wine.

It rolls in on the slightly cooled
evening air;
the Sabbath, a dark robe.

From the chair in the corner
of the kitchen, I observe all the work
still at hand:
the dishes on the counter,
the baby's bottle,
the wine.

If I move to wash up, or to drink down,
will Sabbath scatter like a cloud?
Drop the dark robe
from the cold shoulders of the day?

Through the silhouetted arms of leafy trees,
I glimpse the last glow of light, far off in the sky,
and fly to my last wick of work.

2015

Fermata
for Shannon and Matt

The last resolved orchestral chords,
final resting tones held in a grief-bathed fermata;
rapt listeners poised in knowing silence,
inwardly begging for the music to go on.

November 6, 2015

Bearer

Fearful to be a bearer and never bear:
the labor of love is what stands between.

Words in Other Lands

How else can I eat you but whole?
Soft rind, knobby seeds, and the bitter fruit,
a jewel of the dawn that stings the throat.

As a tender shoot I loved you.
And on the days when the sun sought to wring
from your plaintiff and eager leaves
the last drops of water you were given,
by pail, at last, remembered;
when your spindly arms raised in hope
arched in the hot wind;
I rose and shook the dust from my mind,
and recalled the deeper things
and the yoke that remained on my shoulders.
Furrows grown weedy in neglect,
rejected stones.

How else can I eat you but whole?
We watched as the buds grew
on your adolescent frame.
In the evenings we smelled the fragrance of your
white blossoms,
watching in wonder as that which you are
was being and becoming.
It was hope.
Your fragrance, an enchanting fog
throughout the valley.
                        A call.
                        Across the deserts,
a people waking to themselves and recalling
memories yet lived.
We watched your hope in hope,
and poured water on your feet,
rivulets on your greening bones.

How else can I eat you but whole?
The winter came, and your fruit fatted.
Tender mirrors of the aging sun
caused your arms to droop and bend:
not heavy weight, but weighted still.
The juice grew bitter as the rind softened and
deepened,
and enticed the nesting birds.
I plucked you on Christmas Day,
babe in a leafy manger,
crushed.

Now the godforsaken line the road and dig to
collect what the world has cast on its heaps,
what some call *the margins*.
These alleyways are no longer alleys,
but thoroughfares.
I see this from our safe and distant perch,
and so do you.
I water you with cloudy, fragrant water from
my daughter's bath.
Our time to walk among them may be
near at hand.
You have delivered three final gifts in late spring,
and as we cannot take you with us,
we give you to a friend to tend your dependent life.
But just before,
with the innocent cruelty of a child,
my daughter tries to pluck a half-ripe orb
for a last taste of you,
but she finds you are not ready to give it.
So she rips, she rips, finally,
that fruit from your arms,
She rips it off
                    and between her teeth she crushes

the fruit
and by instinct spits it out.
She says it burns her mouth.

How else can we eat you but whole?

Amman, Jordan
2013

Almonds

green-raw and fuzzy on
the kitchen counter
in a plastic sandwich bag:
a gift from a friend
who did not think he could
eat them
in time.
They lay there,
and I stare back,
wondering how one eats
an almond.

Amman, Jordan
2010

Snaking through villages in the north
at springtime,
we are hunting the black iris:
Iris petrana.
I will gather these rare velvet spectacles of
mourning and royalty
in my shallow basket and then
scatter their beardless petals in the streets
of Ajloun,
among the fallen pine needles of Dibeen.
I shed my tears outside
Palestine—
oh, precious Palestine—
to whom and for whom the prophets
gathered, wept, and died.
We ring you with black
iris petals,
for it is finished,
and we hear in the grey
olive leaves,
a final, divine exhale.

Amman, Jordan
2010

On a Donkey

He is imaging—this
Bedouin
boy.

Silhouette
on a donkey.
Plastic orange
saddle bags.
Picks through
trash
from the gray dumpster
at the curb.
Cats scatter.

Inside his bags:
Cans. Bottles.
Yesterday's apple core
from the
Royal Gala apple
I sliced for
my daughters.

Amman, Jordan
2010

Shepherd of the Sheep

We were all drawn out.
The herd was grazing on the field
at the bend in the road where the cars
speed through.
With a staff and a few hurled rocks,
the shepherd under his red *keffiyeh*
kept his flock in fluid formation.

Then he moved.

We all watched—we, on the balcony,
they, on the road, with dogs on leashes,
clutching our mobile phones,
pausing because of this scene,
briefly stalled by the ancient press into
our bustling modernity.
He moved, as we stood still,
and the sheep followed, marching on the right,
the goats on the left,
and they moved up the bank.
And then they were gone.

Amman, Jordan
2010

63

Marmalade Fear

Marmalade fear, crouched in the shadows:
She has seen me! Retreat!

I want to coax you out, let you lift
your tail higher, and live like the cats I knew
in my neighbor's house down the block who
ruled in easy co-regency with that
woman in the maroon armchair.
Who was mistress then?
Well, I am mistress now,
And I say: Be free.

I am glad that Allah gives you
as many lives as he sees fit.
You will need them, I think, and perhaps more
to get to that place where you will
prowl like a fed cat whose hunting is
her playful pleasure.

Amman, Jordan
2010

I. Riverside

To save a life one must lose it.

I have come tonight to Starbucks
    to sip chamomile tea
and write a bit of poetry
    on the baptism of our Lord.
I have come to do this
                        and
the tawny opacity of the river
    down in the valley
                        thickens
as I attempt any approach—literary or otherwise.
Forests of reeds, like absent-minded
    soldiers
obscure my view, stab my thigh,
    when I try to gain a better view.
I cannot see. Beyond,
                    hear, yes, hear their woody
susurrations—thicker as the languid
    air breathes out its hot mirage-vapors.
I cannot see.

He would yell at them—
        the many who would gather there
        to see the circus of this man
            You vipers! —

(I take a sip of tea to clear the tension.)
(Me? No. Not me.)
(For pete's sakes, I'm at Starbucks.)

Clarity of mission enjoys no better view:

all is still mud.
This is the Jordan.
The going down deeper yet, and deeper—
    obscurity now.
The only guarantee is that
    here will begin
    a death.
It gives anyone pause.

II. Wilderness

Long-forgotten vistas blurred by
    the dusty sands of this day
    and the next
    and the one after that.
We cannot see them on the plain nor
    in our minds' eye.
They are gone; not even to be hoped for:
    only craved.
Bitter craving,
        the silt in our teeth
        the crust around our eyes red-spent
    in tears,
        the muddy rivulets on
    our faces.
The blank sky, divine ambivalence
    to these mundane hardships.
We are asked to remember
    the majestic victories wrought by our god:
  in food, in song, in our bodies, in the tabernacle.
We feel nothing but the sun,
    the thickening skin on our cracked heels.
This god of wilderness: will we worship him?
    Has he truly left us here,
        alone?

III. Temptation

And immediately
mantle and mission given no retreat
but thrust into testing.
Mettle, muster, nettles, dust.
Thirst and hunger—
a day and a night for a year—
wresting redemption of a people,
and a time from time,
among the rocks, along the cracked
        plains,
To show the true source of sustenance
To wrestle the entrenched spirits of
   craving and grumbling
    from their citadels.
To will one thing.
To keep one's feet firmly planted on the arid soil.
All that we can see,
all that is left at the end of it,
are angels and the devil—both at work.

Amman, Jordan
2010

Sons of Egypt, Mothers of Libya

I. Sons of Egypt

Once, in the desert,
a son of Egypt beheld a fire he did not light
in the brush of the wilderness.
Staff in hand, he stared.
The fire did not consume its prey.
He heard, then argued, then
      obeyed.
Sons of Egypt, you have been summoned also;
a fire burns. You have watched
many burn, and they have destroyed
you, your women, your children, your very soul.
Draw strength from this:
There are fires that speak and glow,
and do not consume.
Incandescent purity along the plain,
a new fire summons you, and your women.
Your children's children will know that
such a fire, though once thought terminally
quenched,
has not finally gone out.
Return, Sons of Egypt,
your liberation is not yet fully won.

II. Mothers of Libya

Mothers of Libya!
Your wailing children press their ears to your
bosom as you stare out
the window to watch yellow-hatted madmen—
those who have traded their humanity

for mealy lentils—
move from house to house.
Tripoli is a dishonored and broken mother:
Sirt, bear your blame:
the once-human you raised has betrayed
not only you
but the whole now-bleeding land.
He is no king of kings, but a shoe
on the cloven foot of the devil.

Mothers, remember the Cyrene.
Holy Simon, there are more crosses to bear.
Come home to Shahhat, Simon,
walk the forsaken road that the Mothers of Libya—
the Mothers of Africa—now walk.
She stumbles.

Amman, Jordan
February 26, 2011

Mezze, Damascus, February 2012

They sent a boy up the tree to strip
the fronds like praying green hands,
and he tore them
one by one,
throwing them down to the upstretched
palms of the throngs in the square.

Stripped and thrown, green arms
gathered in a heap at the hips
of the tree, just before its leggy
roots plunge into a small square of earth
left bare by the civil engineers who covered
the rest with cement.

One by one, the tree is unmade and
marchers, grasping the branches, hold them
like flags to the regime,
the dumb and mad.
From their windows high above,
circled in proud rings of smoke,
their blank eyes look down—
thin, stupefied souls that can barely
recognize the symbol.

To them, it's unintelligible.
They ignore and relive their memories.

The boy keeps tearing, and throwing,
climbing higher upon the wooden
cross of the palm.
Mamas in black and brown *abbeyas* reach to
the ground to pick them up.

A press from the back of the square.

Palms—green and olive—up.
Ears.
Waist.

Now denuded, the tree is only wood.
The wood remains,
for a whittler and an archer to craft
the golden arrow.

Amman, Jordan
one year after visiting Damascus

Wind Chimes on a Red String

Returning home to a lively order,
we are throwing open the curtains
    and windows to the air
    we breathe here.
We are the foreigners among locals,
    foreigners among other foreigners.
At least, who knows who belongs?
    Who, indeed,
    belongs?
What kinds of traitors
    live among us?

I am now returning the wind chimes—
    liquid alto harp-bells—
to the spot on the balcony where they hung
    before we left for the summer months.
I had, then, used pink pipe cleaners to secure
    the chimes between two air conditioning units
    bracketed to the outside wall.

They stood ready to catch and swirl
    in the breezes from the valley
    that would swoop across the sheep's backs
    in the Bedouin's field.

We do not have any more pipe cleaners now.
I must use something else.
I find red string in my two daughters' craft supply.

As I finish lashing the chimes
to the metal casing,
a memory I never lived returns:
If the spies come back, would they also come for
our rescue?

Would they notice this subtle gesture?

I am sister Rahab, ready for the walls to fall.

Amman, Jordan
August 2012

She has invited me to sit and
    drink some coffee.
"Five minutes, only," she assures, which I
    know is not true. But I sit.
We talk, and I struggle to know
    what chit-chat to produce.
"Your husband is now in Iraq, yes?"
    Yes, he is.
"There is nothing there now. Nothing to see."

I apologize for the ways of my people—
    absent-minded, insular, and triumphant, and
    therefore, unwittingly cruel
    in our noble intentions.
In my apology, I repeat their mistakes;
    they are also mine.
We can, finally, only walk
    in the ways of our people.

I recall with her the lovely time we had
    at her daughter's wedding reception years ago
    in the sprawling villa of their friend who lived
    near the golf course.
I tell her I saw her sitting, that we shook hands.
I do not say
that I observed that she sat morosely,
nor that her new son-in-law had told us,
    quietly,
that Saddam had slaughtered her husband,
that her son had also recently been
    killed;
that she sat at the wedding as if
    among the mourners.

74

Wedding ashes.

What I say is, he told us you had been through
    very difficult times.

"Yes. Yes, that is true."

She asks, "At the party, did you eat those special
white sweets? With the walnuts? We had them
made specially. They are *mann al-sama*. They are
Iraqi, made from the sap that gathers on the ground
under certain trees in the north of Iraq."

Manna from heaven. I can't remember them,
truthfully, but I try to remember eating them.
I want to remember doing so.

"Yes, it's true we had difficult times. We could not
get residency here. When we arrived, the border
police could not understand why
my daughter and I came alone.
    'Where is your son?' they asked me repeatedly.
    But I had no paperwork for him. The gangs do
    not give you papers when they have finished
    murdering your child.
    They do not issue receipts for their work."

My cup is empty and I return it
    to its saucer, wiggling my wrist like a
    wet dog shaking water from its fur.

"A family I know in Syria, I went to visit them
recently. The man of their family had died. It was
not safe to go, but I went near Easter, so it was a
blessed thing to do.

"We were sitting together and it was getting late;
the night dark. A daughter—she was thirty years
old maybe—said she was going out to get some air.
She was also lame, born with a leg that did not
work, and so at her age, she was still unmarried.

    'The thugs!' the family implored, 'they will kill
you! Stay! Don't go out!'

    'Let them kill me,' she yelled back. 'What do I
have to live for?'

    'They will rape you!'

    'Let them! Then I will know what it is like to be
with a man.' Everyone laughed, including the girl.
She was making a joke. It was so funny!"

She laughs again,
manna from heaven.
I try to do so as well.
                    The coffee grounds have
dried, cracked and sun-baked mud in my cup.

in her house
2012

Washing Cars in Wartime

"Syrian rebels attacked army roadblocks in Midan district in
the heart of Damascus on Thursday to relieve pressure on
outlying rebel strongholds being pounded by air strikes and
artillery, opposition activists said.

"Assad's forces responded by bombarding the densely
populated commercial and residential district, situated just
outside the Old City walls, killing a woman pedestrian and a
worker in a car wash, they said."
— Reuters, 8 November 2012

In the morning, he rubs his palms through his
hair and swings his legs over the edge of the bed.
At the door, like sentries, stand two pale blue
rubber boots.
Knee-heighted waders, he puts them on.

In the morning, he makes his tea and, sipping, walks to
punch in the numbers for the punishing measure.
The tea is hot. Tit for tat, tit for tat, tit for
tat, tit for tat—the numbness is
learned, drummed into minds by
years, obedient generations, of slavish fear.

He marches in his boots to his post,
puddles and soap. The cars roll in.
Astonishing that cars must be washed
during war, bodies of metal,
gleam and polish.
The rain of weaponry makes nothing clean.
Cars must be washed.

Next he marches down the hall to report to the next
goon up. Breathtaking the fruitful efficiency of war
and its stillborn child, death.
Rolling like a wave over the weeping face of

the earth, deracinating life from its soil.
Life scrubbed lifeless.

The soapy water runs red into
the gutter drain. Down in the valley, the cracked
earth drinks the blood of patriots and villains
in equal measure. A green patch of grass,
a bold rebuke that life will not finally succumb and
bow to the instruments of death.
The emptied rubber boots in melted pieces
held more personified dignity in one car washer
than a thousand sorry soles of the regime.

Amman Jordan
November 2012

Dead Cities at Advent 2015

The Dead Cities of northern Syria comprise hundreds of late
classical / early Byzantine Christian villages that were abandoned in
the seventh century, likely because of changes in trade routes.
Before the Syrian war began, Serjilla was considered one of the best
preserved of the Dead Cities.

Do you remember Serjilla?
How we asked when we beheld her quietness,
"What is the meaning of this city?"

I walk among the ruins of Serjilla
of the Dead Cities, alive,
enlivened in my mind, charged
by her mysteries, even now.
In memory I run my hand across the gray
rock of a lintel, tracing the lines of a sublime cross
emblem, a stone daisy on the doorframe,
more tombstone than gateway.

These ruins of life.

They lived here, these folk. They lived,
and living, pressed their olives into oil,
and their grapes into wine,
poured the oil on their anointed heads,
let it run down their full beards
and onto their robes.
At night they fell asleep.
At daybreak, they awoke.
But then sleep overtook them.
Even the echoes of stories ceased,
and every meter was covered in
the silt of a costly forgetfulness.

Pompei's empty spaces evince,

at least, a sense of struggle,
the emptied place of a final suffering.
(For even the dying are living.)

But these forgotten villages were
abandoned, not conquered,
swallowed by what has been called
"the dreadful power of non-being."
Hushed by the slinking fog of forgotten identity,
a creeping torpor of nothingness,
a silence that for a time can be heard,
but then is only still.

We'd whitewash this tomb, if given the chance.
It's our instinct.
We'd hang tinsel from its time-softened edges,
attach a bouquet of mistletoe to
its moss-encrusted columns. We'd try to right
a stone or two, recall a false memory;
let a cheery "Fa la la la la!" ring in the roofless
church-husk. We'd smile—a forced and gritty grin.
We'd wear garish red velour,
and white cotton-ball beards
until our heads ached
with conjured merriment.

But there's not a pine-scented anything,
no nostalgia nosegay, that will wake these dead
from death, rouse these cities into being,
call this Lazarus from his demise.

Now that we are here,
in the Dead Cities,
we can prepare for the Coming.
Serjilla,
another of Ezekiel's dry valleys,

in the arms of ruin.

Serjilla's hope, and ours, is
riding a white horse.
"Oh my soul, be prepared for
the coming of the Stranger,"
who will restore wine to the presses,
whose thigh bears his name.
He comes, armed in judgment,
with searing, awakening Life.

Serjilla, your deliverer
is coming.

Annandale, Virginia
2015
(apologies to T.S. Eliot)

On the Days that I Will Miss You
for Lisa

On the days that I will miss you,
    I will drink ever more deeply in
    remembrance of how we swilled
    great bowls of potentiality between
    us:
how you expected hope to emerge in unlikely
places, so you slung the black strap of your camera
behind the driver's seat of the car you guided down
    infuriating streets;
how, at times, I sat next to you in the car and
you listened to the words that tumbled out of me,
    and indulged my ideas about the significance of
    municipal dumpsters.
And we spoke about our children,
    delighting in their ways of friendship.

On the days that I will miss you,
    I will recall how you wore joy as
    a belt around your waist;
    how you savored small things; ate cupcakes;
    kept watch for the flashes of
        wonder that dart about us.

On the days that I will miss you,
    I will pay greater attention
    to the time given,
    to converging and diverging
    paths.

Amman, Jordan
2011

Made in the USA
Charleston, SC
29 December 2015